D0123636

ELEANOR ROOSEVELT

by David Winner

For a free color catalog describing Gareth Stevens' list of high-quality children's books, call 1-800-341-3569 (USA) or 1-800-461-9120 (Canada).

Picture Credits

The Bettmann Archive — 12, 16, 18, 19, 26, 27; Gamma — 40: Ferry/Liaison — 4, 54 (lower); Robin Harris — 48 (both), 50, 51 (both); The Hulton Picture Company — 7, 10, 11, 20, 33, 38, 42, 55; The Image Bank — 44-45; Keystone Press Agency — 15; Magnum — 8 (upper); Network Photographers: Sparham — 54 (upper); Popperfoto — 6, 13, 14, 17, 28, 37, 42, 47, 56; Rex Features — 9; Franklin D. Roosevelt Library — cover, 24, 25, 30 (both), 59; Frank Spooner Pictures — 8 (lower).

Thanks to Christopher Gibb for lending his help and skills in the final stages of this book.

North American edition first published in 1991 by
Gareth Stevens, Inc.
1555 North RiverCenter Drive, Suite 201
Milwaukee, Wisconsin 53212, USA

First published in the United Kingdom in 1991 with an original text copyright © 1991 Exley Publications and David Winner. Additional end matter copyright © 1991 by Gareth Stevens, Inc. All rights reserved. No part of this book may be reproduced or used in any form or by any means without permission in writing from Gareth Stevens, Inc.

Library of Congress Cataloging-in-Publication Data

Winner, David, 1956-
  Eleanor Roosevelt / by David Winner.
    p. cm. — (People who have helped the world)
  Includes index.
  Summary: Examines the life and accomplishments of the First Lady who devoted herself to helping others and working for peace.
  ISBN 0-8368-0218-7
  1. Roosevelt, Eleanor, 1884-1962—Juvenile literature. 2. Presidents—United States—Wives—Biography—Juvenile literature. [1. Roosevelt, Eleanor, 1884-1962. 2. First ladies.] I. Title. II. Series.
  E807.1.R48W476 1991   973.917'092—dc20   [B]   91-291

Series conceived and edited by Helen Exley
Editor: Christopher Gibb
Picture editor: Alex Goldberg of Image Select
Series editor, U.S.: Amy Bauman
Editor, U.S.: Thomas Isaac Barnett
Editorial assistants, U.S.: Jamie Daniel, Scott Enk, Diane Laska, John D. Rateliff

Printed in Spain

1 2 3 4 5 6 7 8 9 94 93 92 91

ELEANOR ROOSEVELT

Defender of human rights and democracy

by David Winner

Gareth Stevens Publishing
MILWAUKEE

A victory for humanity

On the night of December 10, 1948, the Universal Declaration of Human Rights was approved by forty-eight countries of the United Nations (UN). Its articles set out the fundamental rights of every human being on this planet. These include freedom from arbitrary arrest and the right to food, shelter, and health care. The acceptance of the declaration by the UN was a unique achievement, and its success was due in great part to one brilliant and enterprising woman. That woman was Eleanor Roosevelt.

For two years, Roosevelt had worked ceaselessly as chairwoman of the committee drafting the declaration. In that position, she carefully steered a path through a minefield of conflicting national interests. One minute she would be calming an upset delegate; the next, she would be encouraging her colleagues to work longer hours. As one delegate said, "She was exceedingly practical and tough, though in an outwardly dreamy and idealistic way."

Roosevelt's task was not an easy one. Following the suffering of World War II, good will had flourished among the countries that had allied themselves against Germany, Italy, and Japan. But that mood was now growing strained. Already the lines of future conflict were being drawn between communist and capitalist countries. Some of the countries that had been on the same side in the war had conflicting ideas as to how their governments should be run. These conflicts became more troublesome after the war was over and there was no common enemy to inspire cooperation among these vastly different countries.

But Eleanor Roosevelt was not to be deterred. All her life, as a politician, a writer, and a vital partner to her husband, President Franklin D. Roosevelt, she had fought to improve the lives of people everywhere. She

Opposite: The United Nations was set up after World War II with the aim of resolving international conflicts by peaceful means. Eleanor Roosevelt made great contributions to the United Nations by helping create the Universal Declaration of Human Rights.

Even after she no longer held a public office, Eleanor Roosevelt was a respected world leader. Crowds still came to see her wherever she went. Here, at the age of seventy, Roosevelt is officially met on her return to New York in 1954, after receiving the Nanson Medal, awarded her for her work with refugees.

"She [Eleanor Roosevelt] walked in the slums and ghettoes of the world, not on a tour of inspection . . . but as one who could not feel contentment when others were hungry."
Adlai Stevenson,
American politician

believed that an international agreement on human rights — written in language that the average person could understand — would be a big step toward improving people's lives. As she wrote during the heat of the United Nations debate, "hopes have been aroused in many people through the ages. But it has never been possible for the nations of the world to come together and try to work out in cooperation such principles as will make living more worthwhile for the average human being."

Creating the right atmosphere for the adoption of the Universal Declaration of Human Rights was perhaps the greatest of Eleanor Roosevelt's achievements in a list of many.

"First Lady of the World"

In 1948, Eleanor Roosevelt was sixty-four and famous throughout the world. For twelve years, as the wife of the president, she had been first lady of the United States. She had shown herself to be a uniquely compassionate, yet energetic, woman at a time when the poor in her country were suffering as never before.

During the years that Franklin D. Roosevelt was president, a severe illness called polio confined him to a wheelchair. Because of his limited ability to travel, Eleanor Roosevelt virtually became an assistant president. She toured the country and the world on Franklin D. Roosevelt's behalf, campaigning for him at first, and later, advising him.

Eleanor Roosevelt championed the cause of human rights at the United Nations. She spent two years working out the Universal Declaration of Human Rights. Word by word, representatives of the different governments came to agreement. Without her perseverance, the declaration might not have been adopted by the United Nations in 1948.

7

Although the declaration exists, human rights violations are still a reality all across the world. *Above:* Refugee children from Cambodia represent some of the orphans of the millions of people who were murdered by the Khmer Rouge in the 1970s. *Right:* These Kurdish children from Iraq were murdered by their own leader. Chemical weapons were used to wipe out their whole village in 1988.

In particular, Eleanor Roosevelt became known as a friend of poor and oppressed people. Nothing could prevent her from investigating their needs and grievances for herself. One of the most popular magazine cartoons of the 1930s showed her deep in a coal mine. "For gosh sakes," says a miner, spotting her, "here comes Mrs. Roosevelt!"

Eleanor Roosevelt was not the type of person to simply talk about the woes of the world from the comfort of her home. True, the Roosevelts were well known and rich, but Eleanor identified with many people who were not as fortunate as herself. And besides this, she was a person of action. She could shake hundreds of hands in a receiving line and still seem interested in everyone she met. She could sign and send a hundred letters a day and give each a personal touch. Because she regularly visited one particular mining community, she could understand and sympathize with the plight of thousands of unemployed coal miners. As her friend and admirer Joseph Lash explained, "her relationship to causes and

In Argentina, children look into newly discovered graves that hold the bodies of people who have "disappeared." Thousands of government opponents were reported missing during the 1970s and early 1980s. Eleanor Roosevelt devoted her life to helping people like these.

movements was through people. . . . Without people whom she cared about in a movement, she did not feel she understood it in its detail and complexity."

Eleanor Roosevelt did not value power simply for its own sake. She took as much delight in striking up conversations with ordinary people on buses and trains as in negotiating with presidents and prime ministers or winning a vital debate at the United Nations.

Privileged but unhappy

Anna Eleanor Roosevelt was born to Anna and Elliott Roosevelt on October 11, 1884. Hers was a small, sheltered world of elegance and prosperity. In it, the people her family knew owned fashionable town houses in New York and large country mansions along the Hudson River. Servants, governesses, and maids attended her and her two younger brothers, and her parents frequented the balls and horse races of a rich, exclusive, aristocratic society.

Only once did the young Eleanor ever question her privileged position. This was when, as a girl, she witnessed a half-starved man attempt to steal a woman's purse. The face of "that poor, haunted man" disturbed her for months, but it would be two decades before she would begin to understand his desperation.

A double tragedy

Despite her parents' wealth, Eleanor's childhood was not a happy one. Her mother, Anna Hall Roosevelt, was very beautiful and a star of New York's wealthy and exclusive society. Eleanor was awed by her elegance. As a toddler, she would stand solemnly in the doorway waiting for her mother to acknowledge her presence. For years, it hurt Eleanor to remember "the look in her eyes and . . . the tone in her voice as she said, 'Come in, Granny.'" "Granny" was Anna Roosevelt's cruel nickname for Eleanor. For the rest of her life, Eleanor was left with a sense of being ugly and awkward. When Eleanor was only eight, her mother died of diphtheria.

By contrast, the young girl adored her father, Elliott (brother of President Theodore Roosevelt). But, sadly, he abused alcohol and was often banished from the household for months at a time by Eleanor's

Eleanor Roosevelt stands muffled against the snow in 1891.

grandmother, Mary Ludlow Hall, with whom the children now lived. Eleanor longed for his visits, but these grew more infrequent, until he, too, died when she was nearly ten. "I did so want," she wrote pathetically, "to see my father once more." This double tragedy left Eleanor with a sense of being abandoned and unloved that was to haunt her for many years.

At Grandmother Hall's home, the family still lived a wealthy and privileged life-style, but there were also strict rules and limited horizons. Ideas about women's rights and freedoms were still in their infancy, and Eleanor learned that women were meant to take their place in society as virtuous and dutiful daughters, wives, and mothers. It was not until she was sent to school in England that she got her first taste of a different way of life.

Allenswood

Allenswood was a small school for girls on the outskirts of London, run by Mademoiselle Marie Souvestre, a lively, energetic teacher. This unconventional headmistress, soon to be known as "Sou" to Eleanor, was perhaps the first person to draw the sheltered,

"I was tall, very thin, and very shy," Eleanor Roosevelt wrote about herself as a teenager. She loathed the starchy petticoats and long black stockings that her grandmother said were essential dress for "well-bred" young ladies.

"Attention and admiration were the things through all my childhood which I wanted, because I was made to feel so conscious of the fact that nothing about me would attract attention or would bring me admiration."
Eleanor Roosevelt

11

"To the end of her life, her own 'very miserable childhood,' her wanting to be loved, especially by her father, gave her a profound sense of kinship with all lonely, deprived, and excluded youngsters."
Joseph P. Lash, in his book
Eleanor: The Years Alone

The Breadline, a painting by the artist George Luks, shows poor children in New York in the late 1800s. Eleanor Roosevelt lived in the same city, but her wealthy upbringing meant that she was sheltered from the sight of such hunger and poverty.

melancholy teenager out of her shell and make her think for herself.

Mademoiselle Souvestre taught her pupils that everyone had a responsibility to try to make the world a better place. She also quietly challenged many of the accepted political ideas of the day. She disapproved of both Britain's and the United States' interference in the affairs of other countries. Might, she told her pupils, did not make right; the big nations of the world ought to allow the small countries of the world to run their own affairs. All this was quite new to Eleanor, who had never thought critically about politics.

Although life at Allenswood was strict and far from luxurious, Eleanor thrived on it. "This was the first time in my life that my fears left me," she later wrote. For here, social graces and physical beauty were unimportant. Instead, a critical mind and a willingness to help others were encouraged traits.

A first flowering

With her quick intelligence and natural kindness, Eleanor fit in easily with her teachers and the other

pupils. Her confidence grew by great leaps. Finding that she had a knack of making the shy girls feel "naturally at ease," as a teacher put it, was as important in this process as learning about new ways of looking at the world.

It was at this time that Eleanor also became fascinated with foreign travel. Twice she accompanied her adored teacher, Mademoiselle Souvestre, on trips to France and Italy. Here she learned to cope on her own. She made the travel arrangements, visited new places, and met new people. "It was one of the most momentous things that ever happened in my education," she later wrote. It also gave her great skill in three foreign languages: French, Italian, and German. Her language skills were to be vitally important later in her career as a diplomat.

So it was with feelings of sadness for friends left behind and a creeping dread of the wealthy New York society in which she would be expected to play her part that Eleanor Roosevelt sailed back to her homeland in 1902. And as Eleanor suspected, she did not find life easy when she returned to her grandmother's house. Much of her hard-won self-confidence disappeared when she was confronted with the demands of her wealthy social group. Intelligence and friendliness — the qualities that had distinguished her at school — were not those most valued in this environment. She once more became awkward and inhibited.

Eleanor Roosevelt at the age of fifteen. Despite her self-consciousness, she was known as a kind, graceful, and intelligent young woman.

As was the custom for wealthy young society women of the time, she officially "came out," or entered society, at the Assembly Ball in New York in December 1902. "I do not think I quite realized at the time what utter agony it was going to be or I would never have had the courage to go," she wrote. "I knew I was the first girl in my mother's family who was not a belle, and though I never acknowledged it to anyone at the time, I was deeply ashamed."

Eleanor and Franklin Roosevelt

But there was one person who did have the sense to realize that Eleanor was a girl with both grace and intelligence: Franklin Delano Roosevelt. Franklin, a distant cousin of Eleanor's, was the only child of Sara Delano Roosevelt and James Roosevelt. He and Eleanor had met at parties given by her uncle Theodore before she had left for England.

Now they met again, and Franklin, a student at Harvard University, was bowled over by her shy charm. He wooed her for months with letters and declarations of everlasting love. Finally, after a "never to be forgotten walk by the river" near Harvard, Eleanor agreed to marry him. Years later, she confided to a friend that Franklin said he hoped she would help him to make something of himself, for he was highly intelligent and had political ambitions. For Eleanor, the idea of marriage seemed the natural thing to do, and she was pleased "to be part of the stream of life."

Their wedding took place on March 17, 1905. This occasion marked the social highlight of the year, with the president, Theodore Roosevelt, giving away his twenty-year-old niece in front of a battery of newspaper photographers and reporters.

Less than domestic bliss

In 1911, Eleanor Roosevelt poses with her children.

After returning from their honeymoon in Europe, Eleanor settled down to a life of homemaking. On the surface, her life seemed pleasant enough. The young couple moved into a house in New York bought by Franklin's mother. Eleanor gave birth to four of her six children in her first five years of marriage. Like other wealthy young wives, she served on charity boards and attended classes in art, music, and literature. Yet somehow her life seemed frustrating and empty.

To begin with, she had to put up with her dominating mother-in-law, Sara Roosevelt, who took it upon herself to run Eleanor's household. Perhaps more important, like most "well-bred" young women of the time, Eleanor had no idea about how to bring up her children. After all, that was a job for servants. Still, Eleanor felt guilty about this, but her attempts to do more as a mother often ended disastrously and left her feeling even more inadequate.

This feeling grew even more intense when her third baby, Franklin D. Roosevelt, Jr., suddenly died of influenza in November 1909. He was just seven months old. Eleanor despaired at the baby's death. It seemed to confirm that — as she suspected — she was a failure as a mother, too.

A politician's wife

Meanwhile, Franklin was taking his first steps in what was to prove to be one of the most brilliant political careers in the history of the United States. In 1910, he was a Democratic candidate for the New York State legislature. To everyone's surprise, he was elected to the New York Senate. The couple moved to the state capital, Albany, and, to Eleanor's immense relief, for the first time since the honeymoon, her mother-in-law did not accompany them.

Eleanor Roosevelt set about becoming a dutiful politician's wife. She researched issues her husband needed to know more about, attended speeches and committee meetings, and entertained the many people who visited their home. But she was still, in a sense, hiding behind her sheltered position in society — she was not really interested in politics or the issues of the day. She later wrote, "It was a wife's duty to be

"I looked at everything from the point of view of what I ought to do, rarely from the standpoint of what I wanted to do. . . . So I took an interest in politics. It was a wife's duty to be interested in whatever interested her husband, whether it was politics, books, or a particular dish for dinner."

Eleanor Roosevelt

Before World War I, women campaigned for the right to vote. Franklin Roosevelt supported their cause — and shocked Eleanor. At that time, she expected neither to vote nor to have a career. She showed few signs that one day she would become a hard-working world leader who would champion the right of women to play a full role in society.

15

A poster urges American men to volunteer to fight in World War I. Millions of women, including Eleanor Roosevelt, supported the war effort. Eleanor was jolted out of her sheltered existence, and, in her long hours of work, discovered that she had a great talent for organization.

I WANT YOU
FOR U.S. ARMY
NEAREST RECRUITING STATION

"During the summer of 1918 . . . Eleanor worked compulsively, arriving at the hot canteen at nine or ten in the morning and working straight through until the middle of the following night. The work was a kind of therapy, a rite of passage for her into a world more common, more elemental, and seemingly more substantial than the aristocratic world of her upbringing."

J. William T. Youngs, in his book Eleanor Roosevelt: A Personal and Public Life

interested in whatever interested her husband, whether it was politics, books, or a particular dish for dinner."

Indeed, she was shocked by some of the policies Franklin favored. When he came out in support of women's right to vote, she admitted, "I had never given the question serious thought, for I took it for granted that men were superior creatures and knew more about politics than women did." A number of traumatic jolts would shake Eleanor out of her cozy existence and into the realities of the world outside her social circle.

World War I

Perhaps the first of these was when the United States entered World War I in 1917. By this time, the Roosevelts were living in Washington, where Franklin was assistant secretary of the navy — a job that he loved. The war was to change the way the United

States viewed itself in relation to the world. It made people question their beliefs about themselves and about the way they lived. Within a year, 3.5 million men were in the armed services, and 2 million were sent overseas. The conflict also drew millions of women into unaccustomed roles. They became farmers, factory workers, and drivers, filling the more traditional war roles such as canteen workers and nurses, as well.

Eleanor, too, wished to do something for the nation. She volunteered to work several days a week at the local canteen that was set up at the railroad station to serve coffee and sandwiches to the troops. It was the first time since her earlier charity work that she went to work in the outside world. The days ran long, and she sometimes worked as many as fourteen hours at a stretch, but she loved it. She found herself caught up in the world of everyday life — the laughter, the

Canadian troops are caught in the mud that surrounds Passchendaele (a village near Ypres, Belgium), in November 1917. It was Eleanor Roosevelt's visits to battlefields like these that brought home to her the horrors of war and helped shape her lifelong dedication to world peace.

"She had overcome so much, turned so many difficulties into points of growth. She had . . . freed herself from the domination of a strong-minded mother-in-law who had embodied the values of that society [in which she had grown up]."
Joseph P. Lash, in
Eleanor: The Years Alone

Below and opposite: These photographs by Jacob Riis show poverty in New York in the first decades of the twentieth century. Below, these immigrant cigar-makers worked seventeen hours a day, seven days a week, for a little over a dollar a day.

apprehensions, the fears of the soldiers leaving for the war. In some ways it seemed so much more real than the stuffy world of her childhood.

Turning point

But the war was to influence Eleanor in a much more serious way. In 1919, shortly after the war had ended, she and Franklin visited the bloody battlefields of Europe. Touring the desolate and scarred landscape around Saint Quentin, France, where so recently men had fought and died, made Eleanor feel physically sick. The experience made her a lifelong advocate of peace.

On her return to the United States, she was horrified by a visit to the naval hospital in Washington. There she saw men whose minds had been damaged by the horrors that they had witnessed. The hospital was overcrowded and understaffed.

Eleanor was determined to do something about it. Using her influence as the wife of a government official, she made sure that an investigation was carried

out. As a result, conditions at the hospital soon improved. In a sense, Eleanor Roosevelt had left the sheltered world of her youth forever. She had come to realize that the human condition *could* be improved by taking positive action. No longer would she remain on the sidelines, a spectator to the injustices of the world.

Betrayed

There was another, more personal reason why Eleanor was forced to reassess her whole life and outlook. In 1918, while sorting through her husband's luggage, she discovered some letters to Franklin from Lucy Mercer, her young secretary. The letters revealed that the two were lovers.

Eleanor was devastated. The betrayal brought back black memories of her childhood. With them came feelings of loneliness and abandonment and Eleanor's belief that she was ugly. Eleanor offered Franklin a divorce, but a divorce would have ruined his political career. After a few weeks, and with the help of friends

This photograph shows the interior of a tailor's shop on New York's Lower East Side. The total income of the entire family, working from morning to night, was eight dollars a week. Eleanor Roosevelt succeeded in her campaigns against both sweatshops and long working hours for children.

and relatives, the Roosevelts managed to patch things. In time, they would become deeply affectionate partners both in politics and in life. But their marriage would never be the same again.

Eleanor never referred to Franklin's affair in public, and, when she wrote her autobiography many years later, the subject was still too painful for her to mention. To her friend and biographer, Joseph Lash, she confided: "The bottom dropped out of my own particular world, and I faced myself, my surroundings, my world, honestly for the first time." Lash's belief was that "it was fortunate for the United States and the world that [Eleanor and Franklin] stayed together, but she paid a price in forever searching for the 'oneness' that she considered the basis for a happy married life."

Joseph Lash also recalled that Eleanor Roosevelt had, in a way, grown through the bitter experience: "A woman of strength and grace, she had been humbled. The taboos and blinders of social exclusiveness fell from her eyes." Later, she wrote: "Somewhere along the line . . . we discover what we really are and then we make our real decision for which we are responsible." And she would fling herself into her work for peace, civil rights, and women's causes.

Triumphs and setbacks

As part of the World War I peace settlement when the fighting was over, President Woodrow Wilson suggested that an organization be set up to try to ensure future world peace. Consequently, in 1920, the League of Nations was established. Although the United States refused to become a member, Franklin strongly supported its work. During the war, Franklin Roosevelt had become a respected figure in Washington, D.C. His influence as a politician was increasing greatly. That became apparent when he was nominated as the Democrats' candidate for vice president in the 1920 election. Although he and James M. Cox, the candidate for president, lost, Roosevelt's future looked bright.

But it was at this point that fate ceased to smile upon Franklin D. Roosevelt. The Democrats lost the election. The League of Nations was doomed to disappointment and failure, partially as a result of the United States' decision to turn its back on it. But most personally

Franklin D. Roosevelt was paralyzed by polio in 1921. With Eleanor's encouragement, he continued with his political career and later became one of the most popular presidents of the United States. He was reelected three times.

disastrous, Franklin was about to fall victim to the dreaded disease known as polio.

The Roosevelts spent the summer of 1921 at their summer home on Campobello Island on the border between the United States and Canada. On August 10, after a day of boating, Franklin complained of chills and exhaustion. He felt certain that it was no more than a cold. But the next day, he could not move his legs. For two weeks, his condition was wrongly diagnosed as a blood clot on the spine. But later, it became clear that he was suffering from polio. Doctors said that he would never walk again.

With this, Franklin D. Roosevelt's public life seemed to be over. Most people could not imagine a leader who couldn't walk. But Eleanor and a man named Louis Howe had other ideas. Howe, a former newspaperman, was Franklin's closest friend and adviser. As Franklin battled through the illness and then depression, Eleanor and Howe buoyed him up. Eventually they convinced him to return to politics, despite Sara Roosevelt's belief that restarting her son's career should have been out of the question.

"If she had been less tactful, less sensitive, if she had not always been careful to stay within the limits set by Franklin and to check with him to be sure that her activities were consistent with what he wanted done, her acts of compassion and her desire to be helpful could have degenerated into a scandal of meddlesomeness."
Joseph P. Lash, in his book
Eleanor and Franklin

"A highly . . . capable politician"

The crisis would oblige Eleanor Roosevelt to step out of the shadows and campaign on Franklin's behalf. In one way, she later wrote, the experience "made me stand on my own two feet." Over the next few years, as Franklin came to terms with his disability, Eleanor took over as his political representative, making speeches and putting across her own ideas.

Even before Franklin's illness, she had begun to edit a political newspaper and to flex her political muscles with the League of Women Voters in New York. In this, as in everything else she turned her mind to, she worked amazingly hard. She began to develop her own impressive style as a public speaker. The *New York Times* was impressed, observing that Eleanor Roosevelt was maturing into "a highly intelligent and capable politician."

Eleanor Roosevelt was beginning to see politics as an excellent way of improving the world. She lobbied for more influence and involvement by women in the Democratic party. In 1923, she helped launch a

"Her lack of pride and vanity and her sincere dedication to the public good inspired confidence in her fairness and judgment. By the time Franklin returned to political office some of the foremost women of the time, who had long been leaders in the struggle for women's rights, saw in Eleanor a new leader to whom they could pass on the torch."

Joseph P. Lash, in
Eleanor and Franklin

nationwide competition to find a way to ensure world peace. A $100,000 prize was offered to the person who came up with the best plan for United States cooperation in a peace plan, which would then be sent to Congress for approval. This was a very large sum at the time, and the response was overwhelming. Twenty-two thousand plans came tumbling in, and the winning entry was eventually put before the public for approval in an unofficial referendum. Unfortunately, the referendum took almost a year to organize, and by the time voting took place, the public had lost interest.

Meanwhile, Eleanor had been just as busy helping Franklin recover his confidence. She told him: "I'm only being active till you can be again — it isn't such a great desire on my part to serve the world and I'll fall back into habits of sloth quite easily! Hurry up, for as you know my ever present sense of the uselessness of all things will overwhelm me sooner or later!"

Eleanor Roosevelt was selling herself short again. And in any case, for her there was no going back. She had arrived as a national figure in her own right, and not merely as the niece of one president or the wife of a vice-presidential candidate.

The governor's wife

As Eleanor's words encouraged his spirit, Franklin Roosevelt became determined. Although his bout with polio had left his legs paralyzed, he refused to spend the rest of his life in a wheelchair. He spent much of the early 1920s learning to work around his setback. Eventually, his legs were fitted with heavy metal braces. With these braces and a pair of crutches, Franklin became mobile again.

In 1928, seven years after he had been struck by polio, Franklin's recovery was complete. He was persuaded to return to politics and became the Democratic candidate for governor of New York. Few people expected him to win. Eleanor put most of her efforts into fighting for the Democratic presidential candidate, Alfred E. Smith, in an election taking place at the same time. In something of an upset, Smith lost but Franklin Roosevelt won. Eleanor was so depressed about Smith's defeat by Republican Herbert Hoover that she told a reporter that she didn't care about

Franklin's election. "If the rest of the ticket didn't get in, what does it matter? . . . What difference can it make to me?"

Franklin thrived in his new position, and he easily won reelection in 1930. During Franklin's four years as governor, Eleanor would get used to being a governor's wife. But it was not always easy. Her new role meant giving up some of her public activities. The public still wasn't ready for a politician's wife who was as dynamic as her husband. Together, they visited hospitals, schools, and prisons, but Franklin thought it would look bad if Eleanor was seen to be too involved in politics on her own. So he tried to make Eleanor seem more of a typical political wife of that time period — one who stayed in her husband's shadow — than she actually was.

Eleanor therefore directed her energies into other fields. Along with two friends, Nancy Cook and Marion Dickerman, she had started a small furniture factory, known as Val-Kill Industries, near the Roosevelt mansion at Hyde Park. She had also started teaching at Todhunter School, a private girls' school in New York that was run by Marion Dickerman. And on top of these interests, of course, Eleanor continued to develop her skills as a public speaker and writer.

Black Thursday

Meanwhile, a disaster was brewing that was to change not only Eleanor's and Franklin's lives but also the lives of everyone in the United States and the world. Investors in the booming stock market had been fooling themselves for several years. Because businesses and manufacturing were booming everywhere in the United States, people were investing in stock in an attempt to make their fortunes. In this prosperous economy, even ordinary people borrowed money for investments that were really beyond their means. As long as people continued to make money, however, they refused to think about the possibility of bad times ahead.

But on October 24, 1929, or Black Thursday, as it is called, the market crashed. Rapidly falling stock prices triggered a selling panic. Suddenly, no one wanted to buy stocks any more, and everybody was desperate to sell. Sixteen million shares were dumped

The Great Depression struck in 1929, eventually throwing fifteen million people out of work. This photograph shows the helplessness, felt by so many ordinary families, that Franklin and Eleanor Roosevelt would fight to change.

MILLBURY SAVINGS BANK

Following the 1929 stock market crash of "Black Thursday," many people panicked and rushed to withdraw their bank savings. In the economic depression that followed, millions of Americans lost not only their money but also their jobs.

in a single day. In the stampede, thousands of companies went out of business. Railroads, banks, factories, shops, offices, and farms all failed on a terrifying scale. Millions of people lost their life savings almost overnight. Millions more were thrown out of work. The United States plunged into its worst crisis of the century, and the shock waves spread to economies around the world.

The Great Depression

The years following the crash of the stock market were years of misery for millions of Americans. Banks failed, businesses closed, farmers lost their land. The number of unemployed people rose from four million in 1930 to almost fifteen million in 1933.

Conditions became desperate. People who had once been wealthy suddenly found themselves selling fruit on street corners. Without jobs or money, many people lost their homes. Others simply abandoned their homes and farms and wandered across the country in search of work. These people crowded into the

cities, where cardboard boxes or shacks made of useless material became their homes. Whole communities of these shacks, known as shantytowns, appeared throughout the country's big cities. The people living in them foraged in the streets and garbage dumps for their food. Others waited in long lines at soup kitchens where local charitable organizations provided free meals. Still others starved to death. A visitor to New York described the "hardship, misery and degradation. . . . Times Square is packed with shabby, utterly dumb and apathetic looking men." Everywhere across the United States, the story was the same.

Meanwhile, President Herbert Hoover and his administration in Washington, D.C., seemed unable to do anything to help the situation. The problem was that current economic thinking did not allow government interference to boost the economy and provide relief. In fact, Hoover's secretary of the treasury thought the slump would right itself like a ship in a storm. He even said that he thought that the depression would "urge the rottenness out of the system. People will work harder

Shantytowns sprang up in cities all across the United States, as unemployed and homeless people and their families struggled for their very survival.

"Everywhere [Eleanor Roosevelt] went she asked people to take advantage of the opportunities the Depression offered them to help others, to work for the common good, and to change America from the competitive dog-eat-dog society it had become, into a more humane and cooperative one. She urged business owners to reevaluate what they were doing, to treat workers more fairly and to produce goods that were safe for consumers."
Karen McAuley, in her book
Eleanor Roosevelt

One of Franklin Roosevelt's New Deal programs was designed to create five million jobs by spending money on public works. His ambitious plan helped many of the poorest people rebuild their lives.

and enterprising men will pick up the wrecks from less competent people."

In a speech in 1930, Franklin attacked the Hoover administration's callous and wishful attitude. "Although the times called for quick and decisive action by the federal government, nothing happened but words. This was the time if ever when the government projects should have been accelerated and when public works should have been pushed to provide employment."

Eleanor, too, was appalled by the misery she saw all around her. She instructed her cook to prepare a constant supply of coffee and sandwiches, and she would send the unemployed people she met on the streets to her house to be fed. Private charity clearly could not possibly deal with the current crisis. Political decisions needed to be made.

President Franklin Delano Roosevelt

In 1932, Franklin Delano Roosevelt — soon to be known universally as "FDR" — was elected the thirty-second president of the United States. In his famous inaugural speech he declared, "Let me assert my firm belief that the only thing we have to fear is fear itself."

In the first of a series of broadcasts that came to be known as "fireside chats," President Roosevelt promised "action and action now in this dark hour of our national life." One writer commented, "For the first time in half a generation, the American people have elected a president who gives his fellow citizens the heartening picture of a joyous American working with a zest and smiling as though he had no misgivings for the future of the United States." That writer might have added "with a wife and partner to match that zest," for Eleanor was working side by side with FDR in the great push to beat the depression.

The New Deal

During his campaign, Franklin Roosevelt had promised the American people a "new deal." One basic part of the New Deal, as Roosevelt's program became known, was relief for the unemployed. Through government action, Roosevelt hoped to solve the country's economic problems and restore the people's confidence in American institutions and democracy. Unlike former

26

president Herbert Hoover, Roosevelt accepted the idea that the federal government should offer financial help to the millions of unemployed Americans.

The president rapidly translated words into action. Between March and June 1933, in an unprecedented swirl of activity known as the "Hundred Days," Roosevelt and Congress unleashed a torrent of new laws and regulations to jump-start the economy back into action. The government spent massively to create millions of new jobs on the land and in new industries. It also backed its attack on poverty by setting up a welfare system. FDR was to win three more presidential elections and would go down in history as one of the United States' greatest leaders.

Through it all, Franklin depended on Eleanor's own fiery and energetic brand of support and advice. He and Eleanor made a great team. He was the superb politician and policymaker. She provided much of what one writer called "the conscience of the New Deal." She often inspired him and was always pushing

As part of his New Deal, Roosevelt and Congress spent millions of dollars to restart the U.S. economy. Many people were given work in projects that rebuilt their communities. In this photograph, workers are seen on a street repair project.

> *"I think that sometimes I acted as his conscience. I urged him to take the harder path when he would have preferred the easier way. In that sense I acted on occasion as a spur, even though the spurring was not always wanted or welcome."*
>
> Eleanor Roosevelt, talking about her marriage to Franklin D. Roosevelt

The Roosevelts at their Hyde Park home, New York, 1933. The president and first lady were a powerful team. And Eleanor, in her own right, was able to achieve many of her own goals to help the poor, with Franklin's support.

him for more measures to help the many poor and disadvantaged people. She was also his most popular and effective representative and his physical link to much of the outside world. Where he could not go because of his disabled legs or pressure on his time, he sent Eleanor. This method was a style that had worked well when he had been the governor of New York, but now it was applied on a much larger scale.

First lady

At first, ever-modest Eleanor had been extremely reluctant to go to the president's official residence, the White House. "I never wanted to be a president's wife, and I don't want it now," she was reported to have said immediately after FDR's election victory. But, as usual, her powerful sense of duty prevailed. And she soon saw the possibilities of her new position. "I truly believe that I understand what faces the great masses of people in the country today," she told a trade union audience. She and Franklin wanted to try a new cure for the despair and fear that had flooded through the country in the worst moments of the depression: "We cannot live for ourselves alone. . . . as long as we are here on this earth we are all of us brothers, regardless of race, creed or color."

There had never been a first lady like Eleanor Roosevelt. Previous presidents' wives had stayed firmly in the background, entertaining foreign dignitaries and supervising domestic arrangements in the White House. But that was never Eleanor's way. She would throw herself into action with a sense of purpose, mission, and energy that would make other people's heads spin.

Eleanor the troubleshooter

Almost immediately, she began campaigning on a variety of social issues. Among others, she protested against sweatshops. Sweatshops were a kind of factory known for poor working conditions. In these factories, workers — often immigrants — were made to work long hours in harsh conditions for very little pay. She also continued work she had begun years earlier to restrict the use of children as factory workers. She also supported soup kitchens for hungry people and spoke out for the poor. Through groups such as the Women's Trade Union League, Roosevelt had been pushing for such reforms for years. Her new position as first lady, however, allowed her a much wider platform from which to work.

Eleanor's style as a troubleshooter became famous. When Franklin heard about a problem, he sent her to see for herself. When she heard ideas or met someone she thought FDR should also hear or meet, she arranged the meeting for him. Sometimes it was hard for him to keep track of everything she did. On one occasion, FDR had sent her to investigate prison conditions and had then forgotten he had done so. "Where's my Missus?" he asked her secretary. "She's in prison," came the reply. "I'm not surprised," the president remarked, "but what for?"

On another occasion, in March 1933, eleven thousand unhappy veterans from World War I arrived in Washington to protest the government's failure to pay them a bonus they had been promised. It was the second coming of the "Bonus Army." The men had first gathered in the city a year earlier. At that time, President Hoover had responded with violence, sending in soldiers with tanks, machine guns, bayonets, and tear gas to smash the protesters' camp and burn their tents. A man and a baby had been killed in the process. President Roosevelt used a much more effective weapon: he sent Eleanor. To the horror of her security guards, she went into the middle of the protesters to discuss their grievances with them. In very little time, she had won them over and was singing marching songs with them.

A risky style

In general, Eleanor Roosevelt's security agents considered her style to be very risky. What if someone tried to assassinate her? Under pressure, she agreed to carry a gun in her car. With typical relish for a new challenge, she even became a pretty good shot, but insisted she would never use the weapon on a person. And she never did.

But risk was not one of Eleanor Roosevelt's concerns. When disturbing reports came in about living conditions in depression-hit coal-mining

"During the Presidential years many of Eleanor's best times with Franklin came during their discussions of common political matters. . . . Because Eleanor could travel more freely than Franklin — she covered 40,000 miles in 1933 alone — she became his 'eyes and ears,' bringing him personal reports from around the world. Franklin developed the habit of throwing arguments at Eleanor to test her reactions, sometimes adopting her point of view. As she left the room after one conversation, he told an adviser, 'There goes the opinion of the average man in the streets.'"
J. William T. Youngs, in Eleanor Roosevelt: A Personal and Public Life

From the 1930s to the end
of her life, Eleanor
Roosevelt championed the
cause of black equality.
Above: One of her closest
friends and co-workers on
this campaign was
education and civil rights
leader Mary McLeod
Bethune. The two are seen
here at a campaign
function in 1949.
Right: Roosevelt's
personal style is shown
again, as she entertains
delinquent boys from the
nearby Wiltwick School.
In many areas of her life,
she used her personal ex-
periences to guide her in
her public campaigns.

communities in West Virginia, Eleanor went to investigate. While there, she visited dozens of miners' homes and even ended up going down into the mines herself. She came back shocked and saddened by the wretched conditions she had seen.

To help the miners, she launched the Arthurdale Resettlement Administration Project. In this project, the government bought land and built homes for the West Virginia miners. The goal of this project was to put the people on their feet again by giving them a fresh start. Although Eleanor's efforts were for the right reasons, the project turned into a financial disaster, and became a target for her critics.

> *"What enchanted the press captivated the public. As first lady, Eleanor's approach to people great and small remained as it had always been: direct and unaffected, full of curiosity and a desire to learn — and to teach."*
> *Joseph P. Lash, in*
> Eleanor and Franklin

Upsetting the bigots

A fear of critics did not stop Eleanor Roosevelt from taking a stand on social issues. One of her main causes was black civil rights. Although slavery had been abolished some seventy years before Eleanor's years as first lady, true equality for blacks was still a long way off. Economic opportunities for most black people were almost nonexistent, and racial segregation remained widespread, even in the nation's capital.

On one occasion, Eleanor attended a meeting of the Southern Conference on Human Welfare in Alabama. The seating arrangements, which divided the hall along racial lines, seemed to contradict the spirit of the event. Whites sat on one side of the aisle, blacks on the other. Eleanor quietly made her point when she moved her chair into the middle of the aisle between the blacks and whites. Later, at a higher level, she campaigned to have the well-known black leader Mary McLeod Bethune appointed as the National Youth Administration's director for Negro affairs. Eleanor's public stand against racism angered bigots in the nation's influential conservative groups.

Conservative newspapers poured scorn and hatred on her. In May 1936, Eleanor organized a garden party on White House grounds for young women from a school for delinquent girls. Many of the girls were black. Reporters demanded to know why she was holding the party. The first lady simply answered that all young people like to have a good time occasionally, and that these youngsters were no different from any

"We brought [African-Americans] here as slaves and we have never given them equal chances for education, even after we emancipated them."

Eleanor Roosevelt, in a letter to a woman who had complained about black people in her area

others. Racists — even those in her own party — were unmoved. Many people sneered and called her a "nigger-lover." Roosevelt politely ignored them, refusing to be intimidated.

When she uncovered dreadful conditions at an institution for elderly black people, White House advisers urged her not to speak out about it. She swept their objections aside, saying, "We should be ashamed. I was sickened. If that is the way we care for people who are not able to care for themselves, we are at a pretty low ebb of civilization."

Eleanor made her feelings public again in 1939. That year, the highly conservative Daughters of the American Revolution (DAR) refused to allow opera singer Marian Anderson, who was black, to perform in the group's Washington auditorium. Eleanor, who was an honorary member of the group, stepped in. She then arranged for Anderson to sing instead for an audience of seventy-five thousand at the Lincoln Memorial. The DAR was offended, but Eleanor Roosevelt had scored another point for democracy.

Changing roles

Eleanor Roosevelt forever changed the public image of women. She had noticed, for instance, that within the newspaper industry, women were treated unfairly. Journalism was dominated by men, and the few women reporters who did have jobs were almost always kept away from political stories because politics was considered a masculine domain. As first lady, Eleanor planned to break that pattern.

One of her first acts upon entering the White House had been to begin a series of regular press conferences for women reporters only. Since newspapers wanted stories about Eleanor, they had to give more attention to their women reporters than before. Together with her daily column, "My Day," it was another way for Eleanor to reach out to an audience of American women who had never had such a role model with whom they could identify.

A new role model

No first lady had ever spoken out before on public issues such as poverty and justice. None had given help

Eleanor on the cover of Look *magazine. Through her regular columns, articles, and broadcasts, she was able to speak directly to ordinary people and became the United States' most popular woman.*

to ordinary people. Previous first ladies had been remote and unapproachable, but Eleanor Roosevelt urged women to write to her and tell her about their problems. American women responded, often writing to her of their financial hardships or of family troubles. In return, Eleanor gave advice and sometimes sent money. She had earned much of this money writing articles and doing radio broadcasts.

It had never occurred to anyone that a president's wife might have a career of her own. But Eleanor — overflowing with independence and energy — did. As one writer put it: "To masses of American women, Mrs. Roosevelt stood alone as a symbol of unattainable prestige as well as a benevolent advocate and counsellor who was readily accessible through the media." On radio and in her column, Eleanor urged people to volunteer for useful projects and to become politically active. "Do what you consider is the right and kind thing," she said.

"Both by fate and personal will, Eleanor Roosevelt became the most important public woman of the twentieth century. As much as anyone, she represented that generation of women born in the late nineteenth century who moved from a . . . role of dependency to a new assertion of self."

William H. Chafe, in his
biographical sketch in
Without Precedent:
The Life and Career of
Eleanor Roosevelt

Eleanor Roosevelt also gave strong support to the idea that women had the right to work. Although this was a controversial idea at the time, she would hardly be considered a radical feminist by modern standards. When she was asked to consider running for president in her own right, she mocked the idea. Eleanor claimed women would be "too emotional" and not as well trained as men for such a job. It was long before the likes of Margaret Thatcher, Indira Gandhi, or Golda Meir would prove her wrong. Yet as a successful, hard-working, and kind woman in her own right, Eleanor Roosevelt became an inspiration to millions of women.

As her enormous amount of mail testified, she was a powerful role model. In her first year in the White House alone, she received 300,000 letters. Women all over the country adored her. To them she seemed a "superwoman — a grandmother devoted to family, friends, and worthy causes, presiding at the White House and flying around the country to give speeches." But she was not only popular, she was also influential. Political analysts eagerly read her columns looking for hints about what the president would do next.

Eleanor Roosevelt, columnist

Of course, not everyone adored or admired Eleanor. Some considered her "My Day" column "trite" or dull. The poison-penned, but popular, columnist Westbrook Pegler, who had once supported the Roosevelts but later made a living attacking them, wrote a bitter parody of Eleanor's down-to-earth, earnest style.

Certainly, her column was never great literature. Seen from the standpoint of today's world, some of her views seem almost too innocent and virtuous to be true. In her monthly column in the *Ladies' Home Journal*, she asked people to send in questions for her to answer. Someone once asked her to name the greatest men of all time. Roosevelt answered, "Christ. Aside from Him, it would be hard to name any others, because for different reasons men have been outstanding and valuable at different times." When asked to name the greatest women, she listed Florence Nightingale, Marie Curie, and Harriet Beecher Stowe.

Another letter writer asked Roosevelt how she would like to be remembered by history. Eleanor responded, "There is no accomplishment of mine that I think could possibly be important enough to be recorded, and I have no desire to be remembered except by the few people whom I love."

The letters and questions covered a wide range. One letter wondered if she ever got lonely; another asked how she cheered herself. "I can never remember being lonely, but if I feel depressed I go to work. Work is always an antidote to depression, and loneliness is just one of the manifestations of this frame of mind or state of soul which is the lot of all human beings."

Roosevelt also fielded noncontroversial questions on art, politics, marriage, and even on raising children. Whatever the subject, her views would be unshakably sensitive, dignified, and cautiously modern. When asked what she thought about the then-new fashion for women to shake hands with men, Eleanor was all for it. "It has never occurred to me not to do so. I was taught as a child that handshaking was an expression of friendliness, and I do not think of necessity it has to be limited to men."

She urged readers to study, to go to the library more often, to be more thoughtful to each other, to confront and overcome their prejudices, to respect people different from themselves. "It is wise to teach children that intrinsically every human being has the same value before his Maker, but that the moment a child enters the world he is conditioned by his surroundings. There is inequality. . . . therefore, we as individuals should always try to recognize the actual worth of a human being as such and work toward a world where every individual may have the chance to develop his abilities to the greatest possible extent."

"I would rather die than submit to rule by Hitler or Stalin"

But by the late 1930s, such caring ideas were very much out of fashion in many parts of Europe. Throughout Europe, dictators were on the march and war loomed again. Although Eleanor Roosevelt had always believed passionately in the need for peace, she was not an absolute pacifist. She came to believe that against ruthless enemies such as the Nazis in Germany, there might come a time to stand up and fight back.

"Nothing galvanized Eleanor into action more quickly than afflicted human beings in whom some spark of aspiration and hope still glowed. . . . She listened to the miners' wives and took their babies on her lap. She went into the hovels alongside of Scotts Run, one of the worst slums in the country, where mine tipples rusted and the gully that was used for cooking and washing water also ran with sewage."
Joseph P. Lash, on Eleanor Roosevelt's visit to West Virginia, in Eleanor and Franklin

Traditionally, the United States had been a neutral country. Many Americans did not want to get involved in the coming European conflict. That wasn't Eleanor's view. "I am not neutral in feeling as I believe in democracy and the right of people to choose their own government without having it imposed on them by [Italian dictator Benito] Mussolini or [German dictator Adolf] Hitler." She said she would "rather die than submit to rule by Hitler or [Soviet dictator Joseph] Stalin. The Nazis would have to be stopped by force, if all else failed."

"A date which will live in infamy"

The debate raged in the United States for the first two years of World War II. Franklin D. Roosevelt supported Britain morally and materially as it stood alone against Hitler during 1940 and most of 1941. But many Americans were not convinced that they would have to fight until December 7, 1941. On that day, Germany's ally, Japan, launched a bombing attack on the United States' fleet based at Pearl Harbor in Hawaii. In the surprise attack that morning, over 2,400 people were killed, and another 1,200 people were wounded. Additionally, eighteen ships were crippled or sunk, and two hundred airplanes were destroyed.

In a speech to Congress the next day, President Roosevelt called the previous day "a date which will live in infamy." Overnight, support for United States involvement in the conflict had become almost unanimous. Franklin had chosen Eleanor as codirector of the Office of Civilian Defense and, in the first weeks of the war, she had a mountain of work to do. Her first task was to visit American cities that were panic-stricken over fears of a Japanese invasion. Her presence helped to calm rattled nerves and set the pattern for much of her wartime effort. For the next three years, Eleanor worked day and night as a one-woman morale booster for the Allies.

Her astonishing stamina, which had left reporters trailing in her wake in peacetime, was stretched to its limits. One week, she would be picking through the rubble of bombed-out London, speaking to blast victims, air-raid wardens, and members of the royal family alike. The next, she would be visiting American

soldiers in Australia. Everywhere she went, her presence gave a boost to morale. "You certainly have left golden footprints behind you," said British prime minister Winston Churchill after she took a trip to Britain in 1942. Eleanor seemed to be everywhere, getting almost close enough to every front to dodge the bullets. When British commandos raided the German-held city of Dieppe, France, a cartoon appeared shortly afterward showing Eleanor in a dinghy alongside the soldiers, dictating her next "My Day" column!

The rise of Adolf Hitler in Germany in the 1930s threatened the world with war and destruction. Although passionately committed to peace, Eleanor Roosevelt was not a pacifist. When war broke out, she threw herself behind the war effort.

The tide turns

Eleanor Roosevelt never lost sight of the values for which the Allies were fighting. When she learned that Japanese-Americans had been interned in camps after the Japanese attack on Pearl Harbor, she bravely protested. She strongly believed that the internment was wrong and that the government had no evidence that Japanese-Americans would be disloyal. Her opinion was an unpopular one to state in the inflamed

During World War II, Eleanor Roosevelt, acting on behalf of the president, worked nonstop, visiting troops on the front lines in Europe and the Far East. Here, in 1942, she is seen with rescue workers in the devastated city of London.

atmosphere of the time. But it showed that Eleanor Roosevelt would not abandon her commitment to decency and justice for the sake of a quiet life.

From 1943, the tide of war turned in favor of the Allies, and Franklin Roosevelt's thoughts turned to ways of establishing a new world order after the war. As president in the thirties, FDR had done much to put the idea of a society built on justice and greater civil and human rights before the American public. Now he attempted to ensure that the postwar world would be built on these same foundations.

"If we fail . . ."

Back in 1941, Germany had been close to winning the war. Hitler and his Nazi armies had taken over almost all of Europe and seemed on the brink of defeating the Soviet Union. British leader Winston Churchill had understood that if the Nazis succeeded, civilization would be destroyed and the planet enslaved. "If we fail," he said in a famous speech before the Battle of Britain, "then the whole world, including the United States, including all that we have known and cared for, will sink into the abyss of a new Dark Age, made more sinister and perhaps more protracted, by the lights of perverted science."

Like Churchill, President Roosevelt had also recognized this mortal danger. Both leaders were determined to do all in their power to put forward their alternative to the Nazis' plans for the future. In 1942, Roosevelt and Churchill had declared that British and American "faith in life, liberty, independence, and religious freedom, and in the preservation of human rights and justice in their own lands as well as in other lands" would be given "form and substance and power through the . . . United Nations."

It was a noble promise. Planning for the United Nations started immediately with the issue of human rights firmly on the agenda. As the war ended, the world recoiled in horror from the reality of Nazi thought. Mountains of corpses in death camps, cities reduced to rubble, and an exhausted, grieving continent in ruins were the results of this reign of terror. The people who had survived hoped fervently that the shining wartime vision of world peace and justice would be put into practice. Eleanor Roosevelt did not know it, but much of that work would fall to her.

"Eleanor received criticism for particular stands. . . . Her highly publicized travels drew out critics who were disturbed by the spectacle of a woman making a mark in the world. 'Why don't you buy yourself some stuff to knit with instead of using the army's gas to go on your pleasure trips. . . .', 'If you would stay home and make a home for your husband, it would be O.K.' Other citizens wrote Eleanor telling her 'to keep Franklin company (as a real good woman should do)' and 'tend to her knitting as an example for other women to follow.'"
J. William T. Youngs, in Eleanor Roosevelt: A Personal and Public Life

FDR dies

On April 12, 1945, personal and national tragedy struck. Just a few weeks before the Nazi surrender and eighty-two days into his fourth presidential term, Franklin Delano Roosevelt suffered a cerebral hemorrhage. He died suddenly that day at his home in Warm Springs, Georgia.

The nation and the world were stunned. Millions of people reacted to the news with personal grief, as if they had lost one of their own relatives. Eleanor herself was devastated and felt that her own useful life had also ended. No one had ever given her as great a sense of security as Franklin, she had once said. Now she wrote to a friend: "I am frightened. Who will take care of us now?" And to a reporter she said sadly and simply, "The story is over."

But, as the American poet Archibald MacLeish noted, Eleanor's story was not over. In a sense, it had just begun. For the rest of her life, "Eleanor Roosevelt,

The scenes that met the Allied armies in the Nazi concentration camps were indescribable. To prevent horror such as this from happening again, Eleanor Roosevelt worked hard to promote human rights at the United Nations.

who had been the remarkable wife of a great president, became herself — became indeed more than herself — became something very close to the voice of a common humanity which had had no voice before."

Despite her grief, Eleanor Roosevelt, now sixty years old, began to pick up the threads of her life. She resumed her "My Day" column, offered advice to the new president, Harry S Truman, and other officials who asked for it, and began to plan for the future. "I shall hope to continue to do what I can to be useful, although without my husband's advice and guidance I feel very inadequate," she wrote. She hoped the new international organization taking shape — the United Nations — would live up to FDR's hopes. In fact, as Joseph Lash put it, "she now emerged as the principal champion and interpreter" of FDR's hopes and ideals.

United Nations delegate

The United Nations — FDR's dream — was beginning to take on a solid form. Like the ill-fated League of

Nations before it, it was set up as an international arbiter of nations' grievances — through peaceful means, if possible. But, unlike its predecessor, the United Nations claimed both the United States and the Soviet Union as full members.

Eight months after Franklin D. Roosevelt's death, President Truman asked Eleanor Roosevelt to serve on the U.S. delegation to the first meeting of the United Nations General Assembly in London. She was reluctant because she had no formal diplomatic or parliamentary experience, but she agreed. The experienced diplomats of the U.S. delegation, including a future secretary of state, John Foster Dulles, shared Eleanor's doubts about how effective she might be. They saw to it that she was given a job where they thought she could do the least amount of harm. She was assigned to Committee III, which would deal with humanitarian, social, and cultural issues.

To the delegates' surprise, Committee III turned out to be the scene of some of the fiercest debates, and Eleanor Roosevelt was soon in the middle of the hottest dispute in the General Assembly. After the war, the people of the world had hoped for peace, prosperity, and a chance to rebuild. Instead, rivalry between the two new superpowers — the United States and the Soviet Union — plunged the world straight into the tensions, fear, and rivalry of the cold war. It was now 1946, and Committee III was about to become one of the forums for this new tension.

The Nazis built ovens at the concentration camp in Dachau, Germany, to incinerate the bodies of Jews and others whom the Nazis regarded as "sub-human." By the end of World War II, over six million Jews had been killed.

Clash with Vyshinsky

More than a year after the war, over a million people were stranded in refugee camps across Europe — mostly in Germany. These refugees were from the countries of Eastern Europe, such as Latvia, Poland, Czechoslovakia, the Ukraine, and Hungary, that had been occupied by the Soviets. The Soviets were demanding that the refugees be returned to their homelands and face punishment. The refugees had heard of mass executions and certainly did not want to live under Communist rule.

After an exhausting round of difficult negotiations with Committee III, the issue was brought to a meeting of the full UN General Assembly. The Soviet delegate

"After Franklin Roosevelt's death, admirers as well as detractors had assumed — as she had herself — that Eleanor Roosevelt would gradually fade from public sight. Yet of all of Roosevelt's associates, she had become more rather than less of a public [personality]."
    Joseph P. Lash, in
    Eleanor: The Years Alone

was Andrei Vyshinsky, the toughest opponent imaginable. The more experienced members of the U.S. delegation wanted to avoid a toe-to-toe confrontation with Vyshinsky, so they pushed Eleanor Roosevelt forward as their representative.

Vyshinsky said that the displaced persons were using the refugee camps to make anti-Soviet propaganda and claimed that any refugees who did not want to go home must be "traitors, war criminals or collaborators." Eleanor, speaking without notes, made a passionate speech arguing that basic human rights would be violated by forcing the refugees to return to Soviet-controlled lands. After a fiery confrontation, Eleanor Roosevelt was judged to have won the argument, and the Soviets lost the vote.

A capacity for hard work

The quality of Eleanor Roosevelt's performance had also struck a blow for feminism. Her male colleagues were much impressed. One admitted to her that he had been against her appointment at first but now thought she was doing fine. Delighted to have made her point,

Eleanor told a friend: "Against all odds the women inch forward."

Eleanor Roosevelt soon earned a reputation as the hardest-working delegate at the United Nations and the most effective member of the United States' team. She studied papers around the clock, attended meetings, and talked with everybody. She combined charm, warmth, and a fantastic capacity for hard work, winning respect and admiration wherever she went.

"This I believe with all my heart: If we want a free and peaceful world, if we want to make the deserts bloom and man to grow to greater dignity as a human being — we can do it!"

Eleanor Roosevelt

"A task for which I am ill-equipped"

Following her success on Committee III, Eleanor Roosevelt was asked to be the United States' representative on the United Nations Commission on Human Rights. The commission had been created to draft for the world what came to be known as the Universal Declaration of Human Rights. This job would be a crucial element in achieving Franklin Roosevelt's dream, and it turned out to be the most important role of her life.

Eleanor accepted but again worried if she would be able to do the job. Bouts of insecurity, left over from her feeling that she had been abandoned as a child, haunted her. She had not wanted the United Nations position in the first place. Now she wondered if — without a university education — she was qualified for this one. The task of writing a first draft of the Universal Declaration of Human Rights "may not seem so terrifying to my colleagues . . . all of whom are learned gentlemen," Roosevelt wrote. "But to me it seems a task for which I am ill-equipped." She need not have worried.

The other members of the commission quickly and unanimously chose Roosevelt as their leader. Her great gifts of warmth and understanding of ordinary people's needs would make her more useful than all the academics and intellectuals around her. "I may be able to help them put into words the high thoughts which they can gather from past history and from the actuality of the contemporary situation, so that the average human being can understand and strive for the objectives set forth."

She turned out to be a brilliant chairwoman. She showed herself to be patient and hard-working as she

The flags of the world's countries outside the United Nations building. In helping to form the United Nations, Franklin Roosevelt and other world leaders hoped that a method could be found to prevent another world war.

soothed the differences among the delegates. Without Eleanor, it could never have worked. "I don't know of another human being in the whole wide world who could have done it," said a colleague later. "There wouldn't be a Declaration of Human Rights if she hadn't worked so hard at analyzing what every country and every delegate brought to the issues."

Working out the details

The commission members came from every corner of the globe. Their philosophical, religious, and ethical differences appeared at every turn. Nevertheless, month by month, Eleanor steered the committee as it haggled its way through the details of the declaration, word by word, and line by line. She was determined to find common ground.

Even the draft declaration's opening words, "All men are created equal," which were taken from the United States' Declaration of Independence, caused problems. The delegate from India pointed out that women should also be included, and another UN

committee lobbied for the word "people" to be used instead of "men." The final compromise was "human beings." But just as soon as that difficulty had been resolved, another arose. This time, a communist delegate objected to the word "created," because that implied the presence of a God and communists did not believe in God. The committee agreed on "born free and equal" instead.

Then Eleanor experienced the great divide between the powerful nations and the poorer so-called Third World countries in the emphasis placed on different human rights. The poorer nations were deeply committed to the rights aimed at eliminating hunger, disease, illiteracy, and homelessness. To some of their governments, it seemed almost irrelevant to fight for the rights of a small number of political prisoners in comparison to these grave social ills.

And then came Eleanor Roosevelt's biggest hurdle in negotiating the declaration. This involved the Soviet Union. Basically, "human rights" has a different meaning to Soviets and Westerners. In the West,

"Some things I can take to the first meeting [are] a sincere desire to understand the problems of the rest of the world and our relationship to them; a real goodwill for all the peoples throughout the world; a hope that I shall be able to build a sense of personal trust and friendship with my co-workers, for without that type of understanding our work would be doubly difficult."

Eleanor Roosevelt, on her hopes for her work with the United Nations

"Through her role in the United Nations Eleanor Roosevelt added to her worldwide reputation as a friend of humanity. When the UN met in Geneva [Switzerland], police had to hold back the crowds that flocked to see her."
J. William T. Youngs, in
Eleanor Roosevelt: A
Personal and Public Life

"Beneath [Eleanor Roosevelt's] humble demeanor was a strength she had gained from thirty years of public service — a toughness that was honed now by the demands of her UN job and by the knowledge that she was on her own. When the need arose, she could cast off all pretense of tenderness and whip her committee into line."
J. William T. Youngs, in
Eleanor Roosevelt: A
Personal and Public Life

Opposite: Hard-working Eleanor Roosevelt, seen during a long session at the United Nations.

"human rights" conjures up struggles against political persecution, unjust imprisonment, and torture. But for Soviet delegates, "human rights" immediately brought to mind the rights to employment, to medical help, to education, and to freedom from hunger. Viewed from the Soviet Union, Western poverty, unemployment, and homelessness were serious violations of rights. Despite the reluctance of the United States and other Western nations, Eleanor included rights to employment, housing, and medical aid in the document.

But on one issue there was to be no compromise — the freedom of the individual. The Soviets simply would not agree to the clauses covering this. Eleanor came out for protecting the rights of individuals, while the Soviets claimed that the needs of the state were crucial. On this point Eleanor Roosevelt's patience was tested to its limits. "No amount of argument ever changes what your [Soviet] delegate says or how he votes. It is the most exasperating thing in the world," she wrote. But refusing to give up, she added: "I have made up my mind that I am going through all the arguments just as though I didn't know at the time it would have no effect. If I have patience enough, in a year from now perhaps the [Soviets] may come with a different attitude."

A Magna Carta for all people

The Universal Declaration of Human Rights is one of the great documents of the twentieth century. It is a prayer of hope for justice and dignity after an era when "disregard and contempt for human rights have resulted in barbarous acts which have outraged the conscience of mankind." It sets standards for human decency, providing a framework for the abolition of tyranny and oppression. As one observer wrote, it was to become "the basic document of our times, the strongest, most stirring, most complete description ever of the rights of individuals and the duties of nations."

"Everyone has the right to freedom of thought, conscience and religion," declares one crucial article. "Everyone has the right to life, liberty and the security of person," says another. The articles set out clearly the essential need for the rule of law, for privacy, democracy, education, culture, a healthy standard of living, for the

Robin Harris illustrated the concepts behind the thirty articles that make up the Universal Declaration of Human Rights, some of which appear next to the relevant articles on this and some of the following pages.

ARTICLE 1
All human beings are born free and equal in dignity and rights. They are endowed with reason and conscience and should act towards one another in a spirit of brotherhood.

ARTICLE 3
Everyone has the right to life, liberty and the security of person.

rights to marry and start a family, to work, to seek asylum from persecution, to own property, to move freely, to have a nationality. No one should be subjected to slavery or unjust punishment, it says. Everyone has the right to a fair trial, to be protected against violations of fundamental human rights. "All are equal before the law and are entitled without any discrimination to equal protection of the law," it states.

Article 2 states: "Everyone is entitled to all the rights and freedoms set forth in this Declaration, without distinction of any kind, such as race, colour, sex, language, religion, political or other opinion, national or social origin, property, birth or other status."

The declaration is adopted

In 1948, Eleanor Roosevelt spoke to the General Assembly of the United Nations in Paris before the vote to accept the declaration. This would be the last great hurdle. She knew it was a historic moment. "We stand today at the threshold of a great event . . . in the life of mankind," she said. "This Universal Declaration of Human Rights may well become the international Magna Carta of all men everywhere. We hope its proclamation by the General Assembly will be an event comparable to the proclamation of the Declaration of the Rights of Man by the French people in 1789, the adoption of the Bill of Rights by the people of the United States and the adoption of comparable declarations at different times in different countries.

"At a time when there are so many issues on which we find it difficult to reach a common basis of agreement, it is a significant fact that fifty-eight states have found such a large measure of agreement in the complex field of human rights. This must be taken as testimony of our common aspiration first voiced in the Charter of the United Nations 'to lift men everywhere to a higher standard of life and to a greater enjoyment of freedom.'"

To Eleanor Roosevelt's dismay, the full assembly did not vote on the document at once but insisted on debating it again, line by line, for eighty-five sessions. It was an ordeal, and given the vehemence of Soviet attacks on the wording, she feared it might be derailed.

Finally, on December 10, in the Palais de Chaillot, the assembly finally voted on the declaration. The

ARTICLE 5
No one shall be subjected to torture or to cruel, inhuman or degrading treatment or punishment.

ARTICLE 6
Everyone has the right to recognition everywhere as a person before the law.

Soviet Union was still unhappy about it, but in the end, the Soviet delegates and their Eastern bloc allies merely abstained instead of voting against it. Only two other countries joined them — Saudi Arabia, whose delegate thought his king would not approve of the idea of people changing their religion, and South Africa. The declaration was passed with forty-eight votes in favor of it, eight abstentions, and two countries absent.

Only the first step

There was great excitement surrounding the passage of such a beautifully worded resolution in this international forum. But Roosevelt knew that the declaration would be of no use to anyone unless it was put into practice. Ten years later, in 1958, she wrote: "Where, after all, do universal human rights begin? In small places, close to home — so close and so small that they cannot be seen on any maps of the world. Yet they are the world of the individual persons; the neighborhood he lives in; the school or college he attends; the factory, farm or office where he works. Such are the places where every man, woman and child seeks equal justice, equal opportunity, equal dignity without discrimination. Unless these rights have meaning there, they have little meaning anywhere. Without concerned citizen action to uphold them close to home, we shall look in vain for progress in the larger world."

In the years that followed, the United Nations progressed steadily toward its goals. In 1966, the organization adopted covenants on economic, social, civil, and political rights. Covenants are written agreements that become legally binding on the countries that accept them. Those accepted by the UN General Assembly in 1966 completed the International Bill of Human Rights.

In 1976, the whole bill finally acquired the status of international law. Other documents and activities include covenants outlawing torture, and the creation of a permanent UN Commission on Human Rights and human rights commissions in Europe and the United States. The very latest action that the United Nations has taken is to adopt a Convention on the Rights of the Child in November 1989 — a crucial addition to the original declaration.

ARTICLE 16
1. Men and women of full age, without any limitation due to race, nationality or religion, have the right to marry and to found a family. They are entitled to equal rights as to marriage, during marriage and at its dissolution.
2. Marriage shall be entered into only with the free and full consent of the intending spouses.
3. The family is the natural and fundamental group unit of society and is entitled to protection by society and the State.

ARTICLE 18
Everyone has the right to freedom of thought, conscience and religion; this right includes freedom to change his religion or belief, and freedom, either alone or in community with others and in public or private, to manifest his religion or belief in teaching, practice, worship and observance.

Human rights abuses

Many governments have failed to live up to the standards of the declaration. Indeed, some have continued to torture, murder, and tyrannize their own people while still paying lip service to UN human rights principles.

If Eleanor Roosevelt had lived another thirty years, she would have been saddened by the failures of the United Nations itself. It has often been weak and indecisive in standing up for its own principles. Yet the urgent moral and practical message of the Universal Declaration of Human Rights has changed the world for the better. Its message has filtered out into the political cultures of the world and, as each year goes by, its influence increases. In many countries, individual citizens can now seek protection and justice under the principles of the UN declaration. They can go to court in their own lands or through international bodies such as the European Court of Human Rights.

In areas where the United Nations has failed to monitor or speak out against human rights abuses, independent organizations have emerged to do that work and have grown steadily in strength, influence, and support. One of these is Amnesty International, an organization founded by British lawyer Peter Benenson in 1961.

Ahead of her time

In her passionate support of human rights, Eleanor Roosevelt had been forty years ahead of her time. Thanks largely to her, the issue is now right at the top of the political agenda. In the 1940s, countries accused of human rights crimes would hide behind the excuse that foreigners should not "interfere" in another country's "internal affairs." Few governments these days dare to use that excuse. The climate of world opinion has changed radically. Many people now believe, as Eleanor always believed, that our common humanity links everyone in the world.

And, as a new century approaches, there are signs in many parts of the world that the days of tyranny are coming to an end. Popular uprisings, fueled, in part, by the demand for democracy and human rights, signal this change. In 1989, the sources of inspiration for the successful peaceful revolutionaries of East Germany,

"[The declaration has] turned out to be more important than anyone realized. It's been invoked so many times that it's now recognized as part of the customary law of nations."
    John Humphreys, author of
    the first draft of the Universal
    Declaration of Human Rights

Czechoslovakia, and Poland, and of the murdered students and workers of Tiananmen Square in China were many and varied. Likewise, motives varied among the people of the Philippines when they overthrew the tyranny of Ferdinand Marcos in 1986. But the legacy of Eleanor Roosevelt and other courageous human rights leaders certainly played a part in all those countries.

"We must preserve our right to think and differ"

Back in 1948, after Eleanor Roosevelt had steered the declaration through, she still had years of work to contribute to human rights causes. There were immediate threats to the principles of freedom of thought and speech in the United States itself. There, the cold war had spawned a fear of Communism. Opposition to the spread of Communism abroad had led to an official witch-hunt in the United States. The House Committee on Un-American Activities and a U.S. senator from Wisconsin, Joseph McCarthy, began hounding anyone suspected of being a Communist, being sympathetic to Communism, or even being friendly with people who had once been Communists. This campaign chased hundreds of writers, politicians, actors, officials, and others from public life. Witnesses brought before McCarthy's committee were pressured to condemn their friends and colleagues. An atmosphere of fear spread throughout the United States.

Eleanor Roosevelt was horrified at this erosion of democracy. "We must preserve our right to think and differ," she said. She defended the people attacked by the senator and, in her newspaper column, warned against "the establishment of a Gestapo [the name for Hitler's Nazi secret police] in our midst, and the curtailment of the right of free speech and free association." Few public officials besides Roosevelt had the courage to speak out. "McCarthy's methods, to me, look like Hitler's," she wrote.

Some of her enemies demanded that Eleanor Roosevelt herself be dragged before the committee. "The time has come to snatch this wily old conspirator before Joe McCarthy's committee and chew her out. . . . She deserves far less respect than any conventional

"Forty years ago, the governments of the United Nations made a historic promise to the world: They proclaimed, for the first time in history, that all human beings would be recognized as free and equal in dignity and rights. This was the promise of the Universal Declaration of Human Rights. . . . That promise has not been kept."
Franca Sciuto, Amnesty International

"Human-rights abuses aren't just something that happen a thousand miles away from here. When you see a homeless person on the street, human rights are being abused. When someone . . . doesn't have enough food to eat, or enough money, that person's rights are being abused."
Bruce Springsteen, American singer

The Universal Declaration
of Human Rights has
clauses covering topics
such as persecution and
racial prejudice.
Above: This includes
concern for prisoners of
conscience. Such people,
like this Cuban prisoner,
have committed no crime
but opposition to their own
political system.
Right: Racial prejudice
continues even in the
United States. The racist
Ku Klux Klan stages a
ceremony that threatens
African-Americans.

woman," wrote critic Westbrook Pegler. But even McCarthy didn't dare attack her directly. His power was finally broken when the Senate formally censured him for misconduct.

The United States turns its back

Around the world, Eleanor Roosevelt continued to meet with great admiration. The warmth of people's response to her pleas for peace and understanding showed that she struck a chord with ordinary people. Wherever she went, she was met by crowds of supporters. But her idealism and optimism were not shared by governments.

Passing the Universal Declaration of Human Rights was to be only the first step in a series of international statements and acts meant to outlaw abuses of human

Decades have gone by since the Universal Declaration of Human Rights was passed in 1948. Still, the United Nations has no real power against governments that continue their horrid abuses. In this photograph, Cambodian soldiers and civilians are stunned as a mass grave of murdered people is opened up.

Senator Joseph R. McCarthy. In the early 1950s, McCarthy was responsible for carrying out witch-hunts against supposed "Communists" across the United States. Eleanor Roosevelt was one of the few leaders who dared to oppose him publicly.

rights all over the world. More detailed covenants on human rights, which moved more slowly through the UN system, were designed to make sure that governments met their human rights obligations to their people. These covenants made many governments nervous. Governments are not usually happy about giving up power in any area. In particular, the U.S. government was very cautious about the idea. "If we are unwilling to enter into a treaty on human rights, we are putting ourselves in the same position as is the USSR," Roosevelt warned in her newspaper column.

In 1953, the situation deteriorated. Dwight D. Eisenhower had won the 1952 election and replaced Harry Truman as president. Eisenhower opposed making a UN covenant binding on the United States. One of Eisenhower's first moves as president was to accept Eleanor Roosevelt's resignation from her job at the UN. He then decided that the United States would no longer take an active part in drafting human rights covenants and would refuse to ratify any such covenant.

Roosevelt was shocked: "We have sold out. . . . It is a sorry day for the honor and good faith of the present administration in relation to our interest in human rights and freedoms of people throughout the world. We use high-sounding phrases but we are afraid. . . . our statesmen should feel somewhat embarrassed."

A private citizen again

President Eisenhower's decision to accept Eleanor Roosevelt's resignation from the United Nations seemed strange to many. Given Roosevelt's reputation and her role in steering the United Nations through some of its finest decisions, it was a sad moment for the world.

But Eleanor Roosevelt did not seem to mind. In fact, she seemed pleased to be a private citizen again. She didn't need titles or official jobs. She had become a world figure in her own right. In this position, she continued her commitment to working for human rights and the United Nations. So, at sixty-eight years of age, she immediately volunteered her services to the American Association for the United Nations and launched a new career as a writer, broadcaster, and unofficial United States ambassador to the world.

For the next ten years, Eleanor Roosevelt continued

to pour her powers and talents into work she believed would help others. She was willing to go anywhere and do anything if she believed that she could be of use to solve a local or world problem. And so, in 1957, when she was given a chance to interview the Soviet leader, Nikita Khrushchev, she jumped at the chance.

Despite, or rather because of, the cold war, Eleanor Roosevelt was convinced about the vital need to keep both sides talking. Relations between the United States and the Soviet Union were now as frozen as they could be without the countries actually going to war, so the interview was crucial. The conversation was like a discussion between two world leaders rather than a conventional interview. It lasted two-and-a-half hours and covered the most urgent issues of the day — the cold war, the nuclear arms race, and the bitter Middle East conflict in which the United States had sided with Israel and the Soviets were backing the Arabs.

"Can I tell our newspapers that we had a friendly conversation?" Khrushchev asked as Roosevelt was preparing to leave.

"You can say we had a friendly conversation, but that we differ," she returned.

"At least we didn't shoot each other!" laughed the Soviet leader.

"Life was meant to be lived"

In her late sixties and early seventies, Eleanor Roosevelt's travels took her all over the world. Everywhere she went, she was regarded as a world leader and often mobbed by crowds of admirers. In Yugoslavia, she was impressed by the communist and former partisan leader, Marshal Josip Broz Tito. In Japan, she wondered aloud about what appeared to her to be a subservient role for Japanese women and visited Hiroshima, the city that had been devastated by a U.S. atomic bomb at the end of World War II. She visited Israel and other parts of the Middle East. In India, she met Prime Minister Jawaharlal Nehru. Everywhere she went, she stressed the need for peace.

By now, friends and family thought Roosevelt should be slowing down. But she scoffed at the idea. "I could not, at any age, be content to take my place in a corner by the fireside and simply look on. Life was

"During a normal week, Eleanor received a hundred requests for public appearances. She had to decline most, but those she accepted kept her busy with as many as three or four appearances a day."
J. William T. Youngs, in Eleanor Roosevelt: A Personal and Public Life

*"What other single
human being has touched
and transformed the
existence of so many
others? What better
measure is there of the
impact of anyone's life?"*
Adlai Stevenson,
American politician

*"Her great contribution
was her persistence in
carrying into practice her
deep belief in liberty and
equality. She would not
accept that anyone should
suffer — because they
were women, or children,
or foreign, or poor, or
stateless refugees."*
Jean Monnet, French
diplomat, nominating
Eleanor Roosevelt for the
Nobel Peace Prize

*Opposite: Eleanor
Roosevelt sits in her
garden at Hyde Park.
Even in her later years,
she never slowed down.
To the end, she continued
to live life to the fullest,
taking a special interest in
international affairs and
the needs of others.*

meant to be lived. Curiosity must be kept alive. One must never, for whatever reason, turn his back on life."

And she certainly lived out this belief. At home, she continued her newspaper column, hosted a television talk show, and at the age of seventy-five, became a visiting lecturer at Brandeis University in Waltham, Massachusetts. In 1961, a year before her death, she was still regularly topping the polls as America's "most admired woman." Of her involvement, she once said, "When you cease to make a contribution you begin to die. Therefore I think it a necessity to be doing something which you feel is helpful in order to grow old gracefully and contentedly."

Also in 1961, John F. Kennedy became president. He appointed Roosevelt as a delegate to the United Nations once again. When she arrived to take her seat, the delegates of all the other nations rose and gave her a standing ovation. This had never happened to her or anyone else at the UN before. For Eleanor Roosevelt, it was one of the finest moments of her life.

A life of dignity

But time was catching up with her. Her health was beginning to fail. She barely had enough energy to watch the UN proceedings. In 1962, she was diagnosed as suffering from a rare form of tuberculosis.

Roosevelt seemed to make up her mind that she wanted to die as she had lived — with dignity. She asked to be taken home, where her children and close friends watched over her. There, on November 7, 1962, Eleanor Roosevelt died. She was seventy-eight years old. After a simple service, she was buried beside her husband in the rose garden at Hyde Park.

People everywhere mourned her death. Tributes poured in from around the world. But no epitaph would quite capture the awe and love she evoked as perfectly as a cartoon published in a St. Louis newspaper a few days after her death. In it, a group of angels sit expectantly on a bank of fluffy white clouds, waiting much as thousands of people on earth had waited to greet Eleanor Roosevelt on her travels over the years. The face of one angel glows with sudden recognition, and he simply says: "It's HER!"

For More Information . . .

Organizations

The following groups can give you more information about civil rights, the role of women in government, the United Nations, and the Roosevelt family. When you write to them, be sure to ask specific questions, and always include your full name, age, and mailing address.

League of Women Voters
1730 M Street NW
Washington, DC 20036

National Association for the
 Advancement of Colored People
 (NAACP)
4805 Mt. Hope Drive
Baltimore, MD 21215

United Nations
Public Inquiries Unit
New York, NY 10017

Home of Franklin D. Roosevelt National
 Historic Site
519 Albany Post Road
Hyde Park, NY 12538

Roosevelt Campobello International Park
P.O. Box 97
Lubec, ME 04652

Theodore Roosevelt Association
P.O. Box 720
Oyster Bay, NY 11771

Books

America's First Ladies (2 vols.). Miriam Butwin and Lillie Chaffin (Lerner)
Eleanor Roosevelt. Ann Weil (Aladdin Books)
Eleanor Roosevelt: Diplomat and Humanitarian. Rachel Toor (Chelsea House)
Eleanor Roosevelt: First Lady of the World. Doris Faber (Penguin)
Eleanor Roosevelt: A Life of Happiness and Tears. William J. Jacobs (Putnam)
Eleanor Roosevelt, with Love: A Centenary Remembrance. Elliott Roosevelt (Lodestar)
Franklin Delano Roosevelt. Wilson Sullivan (Harper & Row)
Franklin Delano Roosevelt, President. John Devaney (Walker & Co.)
The Story of the United Nations. R. Conrad Stein (Childrens Press)
Theodore Roosevelt. Eden Force (Franklin Watts)
The Value of Caring: The Story of Eleanor Roosevelt. Ann D. Johnson (Oak Tree)
Women with a Cause. Wayne Bennett, editor (Garrard)
Young Eleanor Roosevelt. Francene Sabin (Troll)

Glossary

bloc
 A group of people, parties, or nations united by a common interest. This term has often been used in reference to the Soviet Union and its Communist allies (the Eastern bloc) or to the United States and its European allies (the Western bloc).

Bonus Army
 The thousands of out-of-work veterans who marched on Washington in 1932 and

again in 1933. These World War I veterans had been promised a cash bonus for their service. The bonus was not due until 1945, but unemployment led the ex-soldiers to demand early payment. President Herbert Hoover viewed the event as a military uprising and ordered federal troops to destroy the marchers' camp. This response contrasted with Franklin Roosevelt's sympathetic attitude during his first term as president. In 1936, Congress voted $2.5 billion in relief for the veterans.

civil rights
Rights guaranteed to all citizens of a country by that country's laws. Examples in the United States include the right to practice the religion of one's choice, the right of adults to vote in elections, and the right to criticize the government.

cold war
A period of tension, suspicion, and competition between power groups. This term often specifically refers to the period of this kind that existed between the Communist countries of Eastern Europe and Asia, led by the Soviet Union, and the democracies of the West, led by the United States. This cold war began just after World War II and did not end until 1989.

communism
A political system based on the idea that a nation's people as a whole rather than individuals should own the land, money, and businesses of a country. Communism's stated goal is to distribute wealth equally and provide for everybody's needs.

Daughters of the American Revolution (DAR)
An organization of women descended from soldiers who fought in the American Revolution. Originally a progressive organization that supported many reforms, it turned ultraconservative during World War I. In the following decades it opposed the New Deal, the civil rights movement, and a host of other reforms on the grounds that they were "un-American."

General Assembly
The main body of the United Nations. The General Assembly is a huge international parliament in which each member of the UN has one vote. Although its powers are limited, the General Assembly is the best representative anywhere of world opinion on specific issues. Eleanor Roosevelt served as a U.S. delegate to the General Assembly during the United Nations' formative years.

genocide
The deliberate extermination of a people.

Great Depression
The greatest economic collapse of modern times. The Great Depression began with the stock market crash of 1929 and continued until the beginning of World War II. During this period, unemployment, drought, loss of manufacturing, a runaway crime rate, and the breakdown of the banking system combined to produce chaos and misery that affected much of the Western world.

human rights
The basic rights that a person has simply by virtue of being human. As defined by the United Nations, these include both civil rights (such as freedom of speech and the

right to have a voice in choosing one's own government) and social rights (such as the right to freedom from hunger or homelessness).

Hundred Days

The first months of Franklin Delano Roosevelt's presidency, March through June 1933, in which he got Congress to enact far-reaching legislation to lift the country out of the depression. The Hundred Days was the most intense period of economic and political reform that this country has witnessed in modern times.

Khrushchev, Nikita (1894-1971)

The leader of the Soviet Union from 1956 to 1964. Succeeding Joseph Stalin, Khrushchev was a reformer who denounced his predecessor's brutal policies and made moves to end the cold war. After his initial successes, however, tensions between the Soviet Union and the United States increased again after 1960, with the two nations almost coming to war in October 1962. Khrushchev was ousted in 1964.

League of Nations

An organization proposed by Woodrow Wilson in 1918 to promote international cooperation and prevent the outbreak of war by offering diplomatic means for nations to resolve disagreements. The league proved successful through the 1920s but fell into decline in the 1930s. In 1946, it was replaced by the United Nations.

Magna Carta

The Magna Carta (Latin for "Great Charter") was a guarantee of some basic civil rights granted by King John of England in 1215. John's barons drew up the charter to protest the king's increased control and all but forced him to sign it. With promises such as those of fair trials and a ban on some kinds of taxation, the charter became a basis for the British and American constitutions.

New Deal

The name for a series of programs urged by Franklin D. Roosevelt to deal with the economic problems of the Great Depression. Roosevelt's plan, concerned with both relief and reform, sought to reduce unemployment, stimulate the economy, and protect the country against future crises. Among other measures, the New Deal saw the creation of the Social Security system, which provides for retirement pensions and unemployment compensation. New Deal measures also provided thousands of jobs through government employment programs, established bank regulatory agencies, made government loans to farmers, businesses, and homeowners, and set up agencies for direct emergency relief. The Fair Labor Standards Act, another New Deal reform, set a minimum wage and established a shorter work week.

pacifist

A person who believes that war and violence are wrong. Pacifists object to these methods of settling disagreements, and many refuse to take a human life, even in cases of self-defense.

polio

The common name for the disease poliomyelitis. This disease is caused by a virus that attacks the central nervous system, often resulting in complete paralysis of the arms or legs. Polio most often affects children. The disease is incurable but can be prevented through vaccines developed in the 1950s.

racism
The belief that one race is better than another. Racists believe that what people are like is determined by the color of their skin.

refugee
A person who has left home because of war, persecution, or some natural disaster.

segregation
The separation of people by race. Historically, segregation has been used as a tool by a dominant group to avoid sharing rights with another group.

soup kitchen
A place where free meals are handed out to people who are unemployed or homeless. During the Great Depression, soup kitchens run by private charities prevented millions of men, women, and children from starving to death.

United Nations (UN)
An organization founded in 1945 to provide a forum for the peaceful settlement of international problems. Although the United Nations' main goal is to prevent war, its other concerns include fighting world hunger, protecting refugees, making medical help available to poor countries, and fostering international cooperation. Most of the world's independent countries are members of this organization, which was founded to succeed the League of Nations.

Universal Declaration of Human Rights
A document adopted by the United Nations in 1948 that outlines economic, cultural, and political rights to which all human beings are entitled. Among these rights are life, liberty, access to education, freedom of movement and expression, the right to vote, access to adequate food and shelter, as well as freedom from slavery, segregation, and torture.

Chronology

1884 **October 11** — Anna Eleanor Roosevelt is born in New York City, the only daughter and eldest child of Elliott Roosevelt and Anna Hall Roosevelt.

1889 Elliott Roosevelt, Jr., the older of Eleanor's two brothers, is born.

1891 Hall Roosevelt, Eleanor's second brother, is born.
Elliott and Anna Roosevelt's marriage breaks up.

1892 **December 7** — Anna Roosevelt dies.

1894 **August 14** — Elliott Roosevelt dies.

1899 Eleanor is sent away to Allenswood, an exclusive girls' school near London.

1900 James Roosevelt, Franklin's father, dies.

1901 **September** — President William McKinley is shot and dies within days.
Theodore ("Teddy") Roosevelt, Eleanor's uncle, becomes president.

1902 Eleanor returns to the United States from Allenswood.

1903	**November** — Eleanor and Franklin secretly become engaged.
1904	Theodore Roosevelt is elected president in his own right.
1905	**March 17** — Eleanor and Franklin are married.
1906	Anna Eleanor, Franklin and Eleanor's only daughter, is born.
1907	James, the Roosevelts' second child, is born.
1909	Franklin, Jr., the Roosevelts' third child, is born but dies seven months later.
1910	Elliott, the Roosevelts' fourth child, is born. Franklin Roosevelt is elected to the New York state senate.
1912	Woodrow Wilson is elected president of the United States.
1914	Franklin and Eleanor's fifth child is born. They name the baby boy Franklin, Jr., after his dead brother. **July-August** — World War I breaks out in Europe.
1916	John, the last of Eleanor and Franklin's children, is born. **November** — Woodrow Wilson is reelected president.
1917	**April 6** — The U.S. Congress declares war on Germany. Eleanor Roosevelt becomes deeply involved in war work.
1918	Eleanor learns of Franklin's affair with Lucy Mercer. Although they do not divorce, the marriage is strained. From this time on, they remain political partners but lead separate lives. **November 11** — World War I ends.
1920	The League of Nations is established. The United States, the Soviet Union, and Germany are the only major countries that do not join. The Nineteenth Amendment becomes law, allowing women to vote. Eleanor Roosevelt becomes active in the newly founded League of Women Voters. James M. Cox is nominated by the Democrats to run for president; Franklin Roosevelt is chosen as the vice-presidential candidate. **November** — Cox and Roosevelt are defeated by Republicans Warren G. Harding and Calvin Coolidge. Harding, who opposes the League of Nations, seeks repeal of much of the progressive legislation of the preceding twenty years.
1921	**August** — Franklin contracts polio.
1922	Eleanor acts as Franklin's political representative for the first time when she attends the New York State Democratic Convention in his place.
1923	**July** — Eleanor serves on the committee for a controversial peace award.
1924	Eleanor Roosevelt becomes active in the Women's City Club in New York.
1926	Eleanor Roosevelt builds a cottage at Val-Kill, near Hyde Park, New York.
1927	Eleanor Roosevelt and Marion Dickerman buy the Todhunter School.

Along with Nancy Cook, Roosevelt and Dickerman establish a furniture factory at Val-Kill to help employ local people.

1928   Franklin Roosevelt is elected governor of New York.

1929   **October 24** — Black Thursday. The U.S. stock market collapses, marking the start of the Great Depression.

1930   Franklin Roosevelt is reelected governor.

1932   **November** — Franklin D. Roosevelt is elected president of the United States.

1933   **January 30** — Adolf Hitler becomes chancellor of Germany.

1935   Roosevelt tries to arrange for the United States to join the World Court, the League of Nations' judicial arm. He fails to win Senate approval. Eleanor Roosevelt begins her newspaper column, "My Day."

1936   **July** — The Spanish Civil War breaks out. It lasts until 1939.
November — Franklin Roosevelt wins reelection as president.

1939   **August** — Hitler signs a friendship pact with Soviet dictator Joseph Stalin.
September — World War II begins when German and Soviet troops invade and divide Poland. Britain and France come to Poland's aid.

1940   **November** — Franklin Roosevelt defeats Wendell Willkie in the presidential election and becomes the first U.S. president to win election to a third term.

1941   The depression finally ends as factories gear up to produce weapons, ammunition, tanks, ships, and planes.
June — Hitler invades the Soviet Union; the Soviet Union joins the Allies.
August — Franklin Roosevelt and Winston Churchill approve the Atlantic Charter, setting principles for the postwar world. Its principles are later written into the United Nations charter.
September — Sara Roosevelt, Franklin's mother, dies.
Eleanor Roosevelt becomes a director of the Office of Civilian Defense.
December 7 — Japan attacks the United States at Pearl Harbor, Hawaii. The United States enters World War II.

1942   **January 14** — The Arcadia Conference ends after twenty-six countries agree to the terms of the Atlantic Charter. This agreement is a key step toward the creation of the United Nations in 1945.

1943   **August-September** — Eleanor Roosevelt tours the South Pacific.
September-October — The Allied invasion of Italy ends with Italy first surrendering and then reentering the war on the side of the Allies.

1944   **March** — Franklin Roosevelt is diagnosed as suffering from heart disease, exhaustion, and chronic bronchitis.
November — Franklin Roosevelt wins a fourth term as president.

1945   **February** — At the Yalta Conference, Roosevelt, Stalin, and Churchill work out a compromise on the postwar fate of Europe.

April 12 — Franklin Roosevelt dies. Harry S Truman becomes president.

April 25-June 26 — The organizational meeting of the United Nations is held in San Francisco.

May — Germany surrenders.

July-August — Truman and Stalin (and, briefly, Churchill) meet at the Potsdam Conference to work out the details of administering occupied Germany and defeating Japan.

Wartime cooperation between the Soviet Union and the United States begins to break down.

August — Japan surrenders. World War II ends.

Fall — Eleanor Roosevelt is urged to run for the U.S. Senate but refuses.

December — President Truman asks Eleanor Roosevelt to serve as a U.S. delegate to the first meeting of the United Nations General Assembly.

1946   **January** — Eleanor Roosevelt sails for London to attend the first meeting of the United Nations General Assembly. She is assigned to Committee III, the UN committee dealing with social, cultural, and humanitarian issues.

March — Amid the beginning of the cold war, Winston Churchill condemns the Soviet Union in his famous "iron curtain" speech. Eleanor Roosevelt criticizes his views in "My Day."

1947   **January** — President Truman appoints Eleanor Roosevelt to the UN's Commission on Human Rights. The other commission members choose her as their chairperson. The commission begins work on the Universal Declaration of Human Rights.

1948   **June** — The Soviets blockade West Berlin in an attempt to drive the Americans, British, and French out. The blockade, which lasts for nearly a year, marks the first military confrontation of the cold war.

November — Harry S Truman is elected to the presidency.

December 10 — The UN General Assembly adopts the Universal Declaration of Human Rights drafted by Roosevelt's commission.

1949   Eleanor Roosevelt becomes the host of her own television program.

1950   **February** — Senator Joseph McCarthy claims to have a list of 205 "card-carrying Communists" working in the government. Witch-hunts for supposed Communists begin.

June — Eleanor Roosevelt visits Norway, Sweden, Finland, Denmark, Holland, and Belgium as an unofficial U.S. ambassador at large.

The Korean War breaks out.

1951   A poll names Eleanor Roosevelt "the greatest living American woman." Roosevelt becomes acting head of the U.S. delegation to the United Nations.

1952   President Truman sends Eleanor Roosevelt on a goodwill tour of the Middle East, Pakistan, and India.

November — Dwight D. Eisenhower is elected president.

1953   Roosevelt joins the American Association for the United Nations and makes speeches across the country in support of the United Nations.

She becomes honorary chairman of Americans for Democratic Action, an anti-McCarthy group.

March — Stalin's death marks the beginning of an improvement in U.S.-Soviet relations and a temporary relaxing of the cold war.

April — Eisenhower's administration announces that the United States is dropping its support of United Nations covenants.

May-July — Eleanor Roosevelt makes another world tour.

July — The Korean War ends.

1954 The Supreme Court rules that segregation is illegal, a decision that helps launch the modern civil rights movement.

1956 Eleanor Roosevelt becomes deeply involved in Adlai Stevenson's presidential campaign. Her support of Stevenson, despite his refusal to support the growing civil rights movement, angers many of her longtime friends. After Eisenhower wins reelection by a landslide, half of all the newspapers carrying "My Day" drop her column.

1957 Eleanor Roosevelt visits the Soviet Union and meets Nikita Khrushchev.

1958 Eleanor Roosevelt makes a second visit to the Soviet Union.

1959 Eleanor Roosevelt becomes a visiting lecturer at Brandeis University.

1960 Eleanor Roosevelt works hard to draft Adlai Stevenson to run again for president. The Democratic nomination goes instead to John F. Kennedy, who wins in the fall election.

1961 President Kennedy reappoints Eleanor Roosevelt to the United Nations. Eleanor chairs Kennedy's Commission on the Status of Women and serves as an adviser to his newly founded Peace Corps.

1962 Kennedy nominates Eleanor Roosevelt for a Nobel Prize.

February — Eleanor Roosevelt makes a last trip abroad, to London, Paris, and Israel.

October — The United States and the Soviet Union come to the brink of war over the Cuban Missile Crisis.

November 7 — Eleanor Roosevelt dies at the age of seventy-eight.

Index

DEP. LEG. B-8.788-91